D1191936

CATS SET V
The Designer Cats

PIXIEBOB CATS

Jill C. Wheeler
ABDO Publishing Company

visit us at
www.abdopublishing.com

Published by ABDO Publishing Company, 8000 West 78th Street, Edina, Minnesota 55439. Copyright © 2011 by Abdo Consulting Group, Inc. International copyrights reserved in all countries. No part of this book may be reproduced in any form without written permission from the publisher. The Checkerboard Library™ is a trademark and logo of ABDO Publishing Company.

Printed in the United States of America, North Mankato, Minnesota.
092010
012011

 PRINTED ON RECYCLED PAPER

Cover Photo: Photo by Helmi Flick
Interior Photos: AP Images p. 9; Corbis p. 7; Photo by Helmi Flick pp. 5, 11, 13, 15, 17, 19, 21

Series Coordinator: Heidi M.D. Elston
Editors: Heidi M.D. Elston, Megan M. Gunderson
Cover & Interior Design: Neil Klinepier
Production Layout: Jaime Martens

Library of Congress Cataloging-in-Publication Data

Wheeler, Jill C., 1964-
  Pixiebob cats / Jill C. Wheeler.
     p. cm. -- (Cats. Set V, Designer cats)
  Includes bibliographical references and index.
  ISBN 978-1-60453-730-7 (alk. paper)
  1. Pixie-Bob cat--Juvenile literature. I. Title.
  SF449.P59W44 2010
  636.8--dc22

10/11   c   2009021151

> ## Thinking about a Designer Cat?
> Some communities have laws that regulate hybrid animal ownership. Be sure to check with your local authorities before buying a hybrid kitten.

CONTENTS

ALL IN THE FAMILY

Many people like cats. Some people love cats. Carol Ann Brewer simply adores them! Her love for one particular cat, Pixie, led her to develop a brand-new **hybrid**. Today, this cat is called the pixiebob.

The pixiebob is one of many popular designer cats. Designer cats are **bred** to look like a wildcat but have the personality of a **domestic** cat. Legend says the pixiebob hybrid started when a bobcat mated with a barn cat.

Like all cats, pixiebobs are members of the family **Felidae**. This family includes all sizes of wildcats and domestic cats. There are 37 species of large and small cats. And, there are more than 30 house cat breeds.

Pixiebobs are smart cats. They enjoy spending time with their human companions.

BOBCATS

Some people believe the pixiebob is part North American bobcat. The pixiebob does share some of the bobcat's looks. However, genetic testing has not shown a link between pixiebobs and bobcats.

Bobcats are the most common wildcats in North America. They live in many different surroundings, from forests to deserts.

The bobcat is named for its short, bobbed tail. This tail is just four to eight inches (10 to 20 cm) long. The bobcat has long legs, large paws, and tufted ears. Black spots cover its pale brown to reddish fur.

This wildcat weighs 15 to 33 pounds (7 to 15 kg). It stands 20 to 24 inches (50 to 60 cm) tall. And, it is 24 to 40 inches (60 to 100 cm) long.

The bobcat is closely related to the Canada lynx. They look similar, but the bobcat is smaller.

Like all members of the family **Felidae**, bobcats are excellent hunters. Their favorite prey is rabbits. They also hunt **rodents**, birds, raccoons, and foxes.

BARN CATS

Barn cats are **domestic** cats that do not adapt to living in a house. Many barn cats are **feral** or stray. Others spend their time both indoors and outdoors. These cats cannot be trained to use a **litter box**.

European settlers brought the barn cat's ancestors to North America. These settlers were glad to have cats on their ships. The cats kept the ships from being overrun with rats and mice.

Today, the barn cat maintains this role as a worker. In return, many farmers provide them with homes in their barns.

Barn cats can be **hybrids** of many cat **breeds**. As a result, there is no standard for a barn cat's appearance. Personalities also vary from cat to cat. Some barn cats are friendly. But most are shy and afraid of people.

A barn cat's personality can depend on how much time the animal has spent with humans.

LEGEND CATS

In 1985, cat lover Carol Ann Brewer purchased a male **polydactyl** kitten. He did not just look unusual. His behavior was also different from most house cats.

The kitten's mother was a barn cat. The mother's owner didn't know for sure who the father was. But she claimed he was a bobcat. Because her kitten's background was unclear, Brewer called him a legend cat.

Brewer lived in Washington State. Other people in the area claimed their cats also had wild roots. Brewer took home two more of these legend cats. Two of her three legend cats then mated and had three kittens. Brewer kept the only female kitten and named her Pixie.

Pixie was unlike other cats Brewer had owned. She had a wild-looking face and spotted reddish fawn fur. Pixie inspired Brewer to **breed** more cats like her. Brewer named her new **hybrid** after this special kitten.

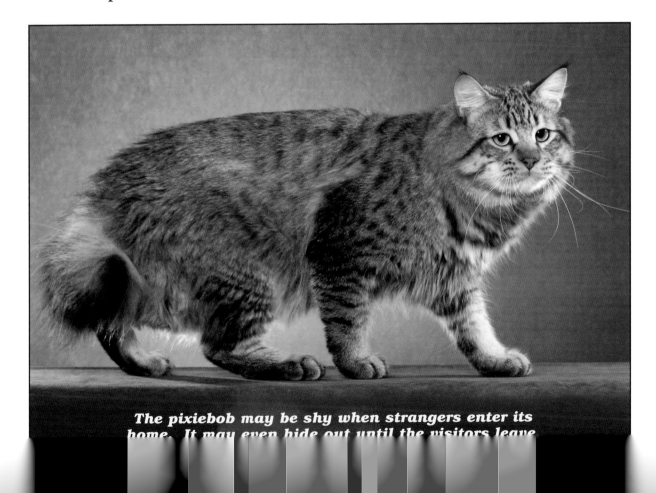

The pixiebob may be shy when strangers enter its home. It may even hide out until the visitors leave.

PIXIEBOB CATS

People once believed the pixiebob was a mix of a bobcat and a barn cat. However, scientists have proved pixiebobs have no bobcat blood. If any **breeding** between barn cats and bobcats occurred, it happened many years ago. Today, breeders keep this **hybrid** true by breeding one pixiebob with another pixiebob.

The pixiebob is a large-boned cat with a tall, muscular body. Its head is usually an upside-down pear shape. The pixiebob has small, almond-shaped eyes. It also has a thick chin, a puffy nose, and tufted ears.

This hybrid's short tail may be kinked but should still be **flexible**. The pixiebob has large, thick toes. About 50 percent of these **domestic** cats are **polydactyl**.

This pixiebob displays the polydactyl foot.

BEHAVIOR

Few people would want a bobcat in their home. Yet many people love having a pixiebob in the family. They say the pixiebob has the personality of a loving, loyal dog.

Pixiebobs are active cats that love to play. Without someone to play with, they can become sad. These intelligent cats can fetch. They can also be taught to walk on a leash.

Pixiebobs do best with owners who truly love cats. These **domestic** cats become very close to their human family members. They get along well with children and other animals.

Most pixiebobs rarely meow, and some never do at all. Instead, they communicate with chirps and chitters.

Pixiebobs
love children!

COATS & COLORS

The pixiebob has a thick double coat of fur that stands up off its body. The fur is woolly and can be either long or short. The coat is slightly softer on a long-haired pixiebob than on a short-haired pixiebob.

Pixiebobs come in all shades of brown spotted tabby. The spots can be large or small. Heavily **ticked** hair should soften the spots. This adds to the pixiebob's wild appearance.

Often, pixiebobs have white or cream fur around their eyes. They also have light-colored fur on the chin. Most pixiebobs have dark brown or black paw pads. And, the tip of the tail is dark brown or black.

Right:
A long-haired pixiebob

Below:
A short-haired, polydactyl pixiebob

SIZES

Pixiebobs are large house cats. They take about four years to reach full size. Males are generally larger than females.

Male pixiebobs range in weight from 12 to 22 pounds (5 to 10 kg). They weigh 20 pounds (9 kg) on average. Females range from 8 to 15 pounds (4 to 7 kg). Their average weight is 14 pounds (6 kg).

Like the bobcat, the pixiebob has a bobbed tail. It adds just four to six inches (10 to 15 cm) to this **domestic** cat's length.

Smaller cats carry their young for about two months.
Larger wildcats carry their young for about four months.

Newborn kittens cannot see or hear.

CARE

The pixiebob needs love and attention. Owners should be prepared to spend a lot of time with their cat. It needs playtime every day. Owners can train their pixiebob to use a **litter box**. They must keep it clean, or this cat won't use it!

This **hybrid** is generally healthy. Yet, it still needs regular visits to a veterinarian. A veterinarian will advise owners when to **spay** or **neuter** their pixiebob.

A veterinarian can also talk with owners about **vaccines**. Many **breeders** advise pixiebob owners against most **feline** vaccines. This includes the **leukemia** vaccine, which has killed many pixiebobs.

Fresh water and high-quality cat food will help keep this cat healthy. Some breeders also recommend a daily serving of fresh raw meat.

The pixiebob needs access to a piece of wood to claw. This will help keep it from ruining carpets and furniture.

Like all cats, the pixiebob is safest when kept indoors. On average, **domestic** cats live for 10 to 15 years. With good care, a pixiebob will be a loving addition to any home.

GLOSSARY

breed - a group of animals sharing the same ancestors and appearance. A breeder is a person who raises animals. Raising animals is often called breeding them.

domestic - tame, especially relating to animals.

Felidae (FEHL-uh-dee) - the scientific Latin name for the cat family. Members of this family are called felids. They include domestic cats, lions, tigers, leopards, jaguars, cougars, wildcats, lynx, and cheetahs.

feline - of, relating to, or affecting cats or the cat family.

feral (FIHR-uhl) - having gone back to the original wild or untamed state after being tame.

flexible - able to bend or move easily.

hybrid - an offspring of two animals or plants of different races, breeds, varieties, species, or genera.

leukemia (loo-KEE-mee-uh) - a disease marked by an abnormal increase in white blood cells. Leukemia is a kind of cancer.

litter box - a box filled with cat litter, which is similar to sand. Cats use litter boxes to dispose of their waste.

neuter (NOO-tuhr) - to remove a male animal's reproductive organs.

polydactyl (PAH-lee-DAK-tuhl) - having more than the normal number of fingers or toes.

rodent - any of several related animals that have large front teeth for gnawing. Common rodents include mice, squirrels, and beavers.

spay - to remove a female animal's reproductive organs.

ticked - having hair banded with two or more colors.

vaccine (vak-SEEN) - a shot given to animals or humans to prevent them from getting an illness or a disease.

WEB SITES

To learn more about pixiebob cats, visit ABDO Publishing Company online. Web sites about pixiebob cats are featured on our Book Links page. These links are routinely monitored and updated to provide the most current information available.

www.abdopublishing.com

INDEX